Legal & Disclaimer

The information contained in this book and its contents is not designed to replace or take the place of any form of medical or professional advice; and is not meant to replace the need for independent medical, financial, legal or other professional advice or services, as may be required. The content and information in this book has been provided for educational and entertainment purposes only.

The content and information contained in this book has been compiled from sources deemed reliable, and it is accurate to the best of the Author's knowledge, information, and belief. However, the Author cannot guarantee its accuracy and validity and cannot be held liable for any errors and/or omissions. Further, changes are periodically made to this book as and when needed. Where appropriate and/or necessary, you must consult a professional (including but not limited to your doctor, attorney, financial advisor or such other professional advisor) before using any of the suggested remedies, techniques, or information in this book.

Upon using the contents and information contained in this book, you agree to hold harmless the Author from and against any damages, costs, and expenses, including any legal fees potentially resulting from the application of any of the information provided by this book. This disclaimer applies to any loss, damages or injury caused by the use and application, whether directly or indirectly, of any advice or information presented, whether for breach of contract, tort, negligence, personal injury, criminal intent, or under any other cause of action.

You agree to accept all risks of using the information presented in this book.

You agree that by continuing to read this book, where appropriate and/or necessary, you shall consult a professional (including but not limited to your doctor, attorney, or financial advisor or such other advisor as needed) before using any of the suggested remedies, techniques, or information in this book.

Table of Contents

Pineapple Cookbook

Delicious Pineapple Recipes for the Whole Family

Pineapple Wonders Book 3

By Brendan Fawn

Chapter III: Hot Dishes   85

Introduction

This pineapple recipe cookbook was created to help you prepare tasty pineapple dishes. Anyone who wants to try new tastes can benefit from this cookbook.

This book includes various pineapple recipes, such as fresh pineapple salads, soups, hot pineapple dishes or delicious pineapple pies. You will find interesting recipes that will inspire you to cook fantastic dishes. You should use your imagination because there is no limit to what you can prepare when using pineapple as the main ingredient. This pineapple recipe book was created to inspire you to discover a colorful world of exotic pineapple cooking!

Chapter I: Sweet Pineapple Soups

Pineapple and Coconut Soup with Raisins

 Prep Time: 15 min. | Cooking Time: 40 min. | Servings: 4

Ingredients:

1 fresh pineapple

2 cups of raisins

5 tablespoons coconut oil

4 cups of water

4 oz noodles

1 cup of white flour

2 tablespoons sugar

1 cup of coconut milk

salt

How to Cook:

1. Peel and cut the pineapple into small cubes or use canned pineapple.

2. Wash and soak the raisins in the warm water for around 10-20 minutes.

3. In a pan, boil the pineapple for around 10-15 minutes until the pineapple is soft.

4. Mash the pineapple using a blender, food processor or potato masher until the creamy consistency and homogenous mass.

5. Boil the water and cook the noodles for 15 minutes or follow the cooking time suggested on the packet.

6. In a saucepan, combine the water, coconut oil, coconut milk, pineapples, noodles, white flour, sugar, raisins and salt and then cook for 10 minutes to serve warm.

Nutritional Information:

Calories: 115; Total fat: 8 oz; Total carbohydrates: 16 oz; Protein: 7.5 oz

Pineapple Soup with Raisins and Apricots

 Prep Time: 15 min. | Cooking Time: 35 min. | Servings: 4

Ingredients:

1 fresh pineapple

2 cups of raisins

2 cups of apricots, dried

5 tablespoons coconut oil

4 cups of water

4 oz noodles

1 cup of white flour

2 tablespoons sugar

1 cup of coconut milk

salt

How to Cook:

1. Peel and cut the pineapple into small cubes or use canned pineapple.

2. Wash and soak the raisins and apricots in the warm water for around 10-20 minutes. Then cube or chop the apricots.

3. In a pan, boil the pineapple for around 10-15 minutes until the pineapple is soft and mix in the raisins and apricots.

4. Mash the pineapple using a blender, food processor or potato masher until the creamy consistency and homogenous mass.

5. Boil the water and cook the noodles for 15 minutes or follow the cooking time suggested on the packet.

6. In a saucepan, combine the water, coconut oil, coconut milk, pineapples, noodles, white flour, sugar, raisins, apricots, and salt and then cook for 10 minutes to serve warm.

Nutritional Information:

Calories: 116; Total fat: 9 oz; Total carbohydrates: 16.5 oz; Protein:
7 oz

Pineapple and Oat Soup

Prep Time: 15 min. | Cooking Time: 45 min. | Servings: 4

Ingredients:

1 fresh pineapple

2 cups of oats

2 cups of raisins

5 tablespoons sesame seeds oil

1 cup of white flour

4 tablespoons sugar

1 cup of oat milk

salt

How to Cook:

1. Peel and cut the pineapple into small cubes or use canned pineapple.

2. Wash and soak the raisins in the warm water for around 10-20 minutes. Soak the oats for overnight.

3. In a pan, boil the pineapple for around 10-15 minutes until the pineapple is soft.

4. Mash the pineapple, oats, and raisins using a blender, food processor or potato masher until the creamy consistency and homogenous mass.

5. In a saucepan, combine the sesame seeds oil, oat milk, pineapple mixture, white flour, sugar, and salt, and then cook for around 10 minutes to serve warm.

Nutritional Information:

Calories: 119; Total fat: 10 oz; Total carbohydrates: 17 oz; Protein: 8 oz

Pineapple Soup with Oranges and Walnuts

 Prep Time: 15 min. | Cooking Time: 45 min. | Servings: 4

Ingredients:

1 fresh pineapple

2 cups of oranges, cubed

2 cups of walnuts

5 tablespoons coconut oil

1 cup of white flour

4 tablespoons sugar

1 cup of oat milk

1 tablespoon pumpkin seeds

salt

How to Cook:

1. Peel and cut the pineapple into small cubes or use canned pineapples.

2. Preheat the oven to 250°- 270° Fahrenheit and roast the walnuts in the oven for 10 minutes until lightly browned and crispy and then set aside to cool completely. Then grind the walnuts using a food processor or blender.

3. In a pan, boil the pineapple for around 10-15 minutes until the pineapple is soft.

4. Mash the pineapple using a blender, food processor or potato masher until the creamy consistency and homogenous mass.

5. In a saucepan, combine the coconut oil, oat milk, pineapple, cubed oranges, walnuts, white flour, sugar and salt, and then cook for around 10 minutes to serve warm with the pumpkin seeds.

Nutritional Information:

Calories: 120; Total fat: 12 oz; Total carbohydrates: 18 oz; Protein: 10 oz

Pineapple Soup with Plums

 Prep Time: 15 min. | Cooking Time: 50 min. | Servings: 4

Ingredients:

1 fresh pineapple, peeled and cubed

1 cup of plums, dried

1 cup of raisins

2 cups of coconut milk

1 cup of white flour

4 tablespoons brown sugar

How to Cook:

1. Wash and soak the plums and raisins in the warm water for around 10-30 minutes and then chop the dried fruits.

2. Pour the water and boil the pineapple for 15 minutes until soft.

3. In a pan, mash the pineapple and carrots using a potato masher or blender until creamy consistency and homogenous mass.

4. In a saucepan, combine the water, mashed pineapple, chopped plums, raisins, white flour, brown sugar, coconut milk, and then cook for 10 minutes to serve warm.

Nutritional Information:

Calories: 142; Total fat: 13 oz; Total carbohydrates: 23 oz; Protein: 9 oz

Pineapple Strawberry Soup

 Prep Time: 15 min. | Cooking Time: 35 min. | Servings: 4

Ingredients:

1 fresh pineapple, peeled and cubed

2 cups of strawberry jam

1 cup of oats

4 cups of water

2 cups of oat milk

1 cup of white flour

3 tablespoons sugar

3 tablespoons liquid honey

How to Cook:

1. Soak the oats in the warm water for 30 minutes and then boil the pineapple for 15-20 minutes until tender.

2. In a pan, combine the pineapple and strawberry jam with the sugar and honey and then mash using a potato masher or blender until creamy consistency and homogenous mass.

3. In a saucepan, combine the mashed pineapple with the strawberry jam, oats, white flour, sugar, oat milk, honey and then cook for 10 minutes. Serve warm with the fresh strawberries.

Nutritional Information:

Calories: 139; Total fat: 13.8 oz; Total carbohydrates: 23 oz; Protein: 9 oz

Summer Pineapple and Cherry Soup

Prep Time: 15 min. | Cooking Time: 45 min. | Servings: 4

Ingredients:

1 fresh pineapple, peeled and cubed

2 cups of fresh cherries, pitted

1 cup of cherry jam

1 cup of potato starch

3 tablespoons sugar

3 tablespoons liquid honey

How to Cook:

1. Boil the pineapple for 15-20 minutes until tender. In the same saucepan boil the potato starch and sugar over low heat for around 15 minutes, stirring all the time with a spoon until sugar dissolves.

2. Combine the pineapple with the cherry jam, cherries, and honey and then mash the fruits using a potato masher or blender until creamy consistency and homogenous mass.

3. In a saucepan, combine the mashed pineapple, cherry jam, cherries, honey, potato starch with the sugar, add some water and then boil for 10 minutes. Serve warm with the fresh cherries.

Nutritional Information:

Calories: 142; Total fat: 14 oz; Total carbohydrates: 24 oz; Protein: 10 oz

Summer Pineapple Soup with Strawberries

Prep Time: 15 min. | Cooking Time: 45 min. | Servings: 4

Ingredients:

1 fresh pineapple, peeled and cubed

2 cups of fresh strawberries

1 cup of strawberry jam

1 cup of potato starch

3 tablespoons sugar

3 tablespoons liquid honey

How to Cook:

1. Boil the pineapple for 15-20 minutes until tender. In the same saucepan boil the potato starch and sugar over low heat for around 15 minutes, stirring all the time with a spoon until sugar dissolves.

2. Combine the pineapple with the strawberry jam, strawberries, and honey and then mash the fruits using a potato masher or blender until creamy consistency and homogenous mass.

3. In a saucepan, combine the mashed pineapple, strawberry jam, strawberries, honey, potato starch with the sugar, add some water and then boil for 10 minutes. Serve warm with the fresh berries.

Nutritional Information:

Calories: 143; Total fat: 14.5 oz; Total carbohydrates: 23 oz; Protein: 11 oz

Summer Pineapple and Blueberry Soup

 Prep Time: 15 min. | Cooking Time: 45 min. | Servings: 4

Ingredients:

1 fresh pineapple, peeled and cubed

2 cups of fresh blueberries

1 cup of blueberry jam

1 cup of potato starch

4 tablespoons sugar

3 tablespoons liquid honey

How to Cook:

1. Boil the pineapple for 15-20 minutes until tender. In the same saucepan boil the potato starch and sugar over low heat for around 15 minutes, stirring all the time with a spoon until sugar dissolves.

2. Meanwhile, combine the blueberries with the sugar and mash using a potato masher.

3. Combine the pineapple cubes with the blueberry jam, mashed blueberries, and honey and then mash the fruits using a potato masher or blender until creamy consistency and homogenous mass.

4. In a saucepan, combine the mashed pineapple, blueberry jam, blueberries, honey, and potato starch with the sugar and add some water and then boil for 10 minutes. Serve warm with the spray cream.

Nutritional Information:

Calories: 142; Total fat: 14 oz; Total carbohydrates: 24 oz; Protein: 10 oz

Summer Pineapple and Gooseberry Soup

 Prep Time: 15 min. | Cooking Time: 45 min. | Servings: 4

Ingredients:

1 fresh pineapple, peeled and cubed

2 cups of fresh gooseberries

1 cup of gooseberry jam

1 cup of potato starch

4 tablespoons sugar

3 tablespoons liquid honey

How to Cook:

1. Boil the pineapple for 15-20 minutes until tender. In the same saucepan boil the potato starch and sugar over low heat for around 15 minutes, stirring all the time with a spoon until sugar dissolves.

2. Combine the pineapple with the gooseberry jam, gooseberries, and honey and then mash the fruits using a potato masher or blender until creamy consistency and homogenous mass.

3. In a saucepan, combine the mashed pineapple, gooseberry jam, gooseberries, honey, potato starch with the sugar, add some water and then boil for 10 minutes. Serve warm with the spray cream.

Nutritional Information:

Calories: 142; Total fat: 14 oz; Total carbohydrates: 24 oz; Protein: 10 oz

Chapter II: Pineapple Salads

Pineapple and Mango Salad with Lemons and Oranges

 *Prep. Time: 20 min. | Servings: 2*

Ingredients:

1 can of canned pineapples, cubed

2 cups of oranges, cubed

1 mango, peeled and cubed

1 cup of raisins

5 tablespoons lemon juice, freshly squeezed

10 spinach leaves

Dressing:

5 tablespoons maple syrup

1 teaspoon pure vanilla extract

½ teaspoon cinnamon

How to Prepare:

1. Wash and soak the raisins in the warm water for 10-20 minutes.

2. Combine the cubed pineapple with the cubed oranges, cubed mango, and raisins.

3. Now let's start the dressing by combining the maple syrup, pure vanilla extract, and cinnamon. Don't forget to mix well until smooth consistency and then set aside.

4. Meanwhile, squeeze the orange to get the fresh and fragrant orange juice.

5. Pour the lemon juice and the sweet salad dressing over the pineapple and mango salad and mix well. Then add the spinach leaves on top and cover the bowl to place the salad in the fridge for few hours.

Nutritional Information:

Calories: 127; Total fat: 15 oz; Total carbohydrates: 28 oz; Protein: 8 oz

Pineapple and Mango Salad with Strawberries

 Prep. Time: 15 min. | Servings: 2

Ingredients:

1 can of canned pineapples, cubed

1 cup of small and sweet strawberries, halved

1 mango, peeled and cubed

1 cup of raisins

3 tablespoons lemon juice, freshly squeezed

1 lemon, chopped

10 spinach leaves

Dressing:

5 tablespoons maple syrup

1 teaspoon pure vanilla extract

½ teaspoon cinnamon

How to Prepare:

1. Wash and soak the raisins in the warm water for 10-20 minutes.
2. Combine the cubed pineapple with the halved strawberries, cubed mango, and raisins and mix in the chopped lemon.
3. Now let's start the dressing by combining the maple syrup, pure vanilla extract, and cinnamon. Don't forget to mix well until smooth consistency and then set aside.
4. Meanwhile, squeeze the lemon to get the fresh and fragrant lemon juice.
5. Pour the lemon juice and the sweet salad dressing over the pineapple and mango salad and mix well. Then add the spinach leaves on top and cover the bowl to place the salad in the fridge for few hours.

Nutritional Information:

Calories: 129; Total fat: 14 oz; Total carbohydrates: 27 oz; Protein: 7 oz

Pineapple and Mango Salad with Apples

 Prep. Time: 15 min. | Servings: 2

Ingredients:

1 can of canned or fresh pineapple, cubed

2 cups of sour apples, peeled and cubed

1 mango, peeled and cubed

1 cup of raisins

4 tablespoons lemon juice, freshly squeezed

10 spinach leaves

Dressing:

5 tablespoons maple syrup

1 teaspoon pure vanilla extract

½ teaspoon cinnamon

How to Prepare:

1. Wash and soak the raisins in the warm water for 10-20 minutes.

2. Combine the cubed pineapple with the cubed apples, cubed mango, and washed raisins.

3. Now let's start the dressing by combining the maple syrup, pure vanilla extract, and cinnamon. Don't forget to mix well until smooth consistency and then set aside.

4. Meanwhile, squeeze the lemon o get the fresh and fragrant lemon juice.

5. Pour the lemon juice and the sweet salad dressing over the pineapple and mango salad with apples and mix well. Then add in the spinach leaves on top and cover the bowl to place the salad in the fridge for few hours.

Nutritional Information:

Calories: 127; Total fat: 15 oz; Total carbohydrates: 29 oz; Protein: 7.5 oz

Pineapple and Mango Salad with Pears

 Prep. Time: 30 min. | Servings: 2

Ingredients:

1 can of canned or fresh pineapple, cubed

2 cups of sweet and juicy pears, peeled and cubed (the best choice

for this salad is Doyenne du Comice or Bosc)

1 mango, peeled and cubed

1 cup of raisins

4 tablespoons lemon juice, freshly squeezed

Dressing:

5 tablespoons sugar

1 teaspoon pure vanilla extract

½ teaspoon cinnamon

canned pineapple juice

How to Prepare:

1. Wash and soak the raisins in the warm water for 10-20
   minutes.

2. Combine the cubed pineapple with the cubed pears, cubed mango, and washed raisins.

1. Now let's start the dressing by combining the sugar, pure vanilla extract, cinnamon, and pineapple juice. Stir until the sugar dissolves completely and you get the smooth consistency. Taste some mixture using a spoon or a scoop. You shouldn't see or feel any sugar crystals in the spoon, in your mouth or on your tongue. Keep stirring and tasting for few minutes.

3. Meanwhile, squeeze the lemon to get the fresh and fragrant lemon juice.

4. Pour the lemon juice and the sweet salad dressing over the pineapple and mango salad with pears and mix well. Then cover the bowl to place the salad in the fridge for few hours.

Nutritional Information:

Calories: 130; Total fat: 16 oz; Total carbohydrates: 30 oz; Protein: 9 oz

Pineapple Salad with Avocado and Apples

 Prep. Time: 30 min. | *Servings: 2*

Ingredients:

1 can of canned or fresh pineapple, cubed

2 cups of sour and crispy apples, peeled and cubed (the best choice

for this salad are Fuji or Gala apples)

1 avocado, peeled and cubed

1 cup of raisins

4 tablespoons lemon juice, freshly squeezed

Dressing:

5 tablespoons sugar

1 teaspoon pure vanilla extract

½ teaspoon cinnamon

canned pineapple juice

How to Prepare:

1. Wash and soak the raisins in the warm water for 10-20 minutes.

2. Combine the cubed pineapple with the cubed apples, cubed avocado, and washed raisins.

2. Now let's start the dressing by combining the sugar, pure vanilla extract, cinnamon, and pineapple juice. Stir until the sugar dissolves completely and you get the smooth consistency. Taste some mixture using a spoon or a scoop. You shouldn't see or feel any sugar crystals in the spoon, in your mouth or on your tongue. Keep stirring and tasting for few minutes.

3. Meanwhile, squeeze the lemon to get the fresh and fragrant lemon juice.

4. Pour the lemon juice and the sweet salad dressing over the pineapple salad with avocado and apples and mix well. Then cover the bowl to place the salad in the fridge for few hours.

Nutritional Information:

Calories: 145; Total fat: 24 oz; Total carbohydrates: 38 oz; Protein: 13 oz

Pineapple Salad with Avocado and Celery

 Prep. Time: 30 min. | Servings: 2

Ingredients:

1 can of canned or fresh pineapple, cubed

2 cups of crispy and juicy celery stalks cubed

1 avocado, peeled and cubed

1 cup of raisins

Dressing:

canned pineapple juice

1 tablespoon brown sugar

4 tablespoons lemon juice, freshly squeezed

How to Prepare:

3. Wash and soak the raisins in the warm water for 10-20 minutes.

4. Combine the cubed pineapple with the cubed celery stalks, cubed avocado, and washed raisins.

5. Now let's start the dressing by combining the pineapple juice, brown sugar, and lemon juice. Stir until the sugar dissolves completely and you get the smooth consistency.

Taste some mixture using a spoon or a scoop. You shouldn't see or feel any sugar crystals in the spoon, in your mouth or on your tongue. Keep stirring and tasting for few minutes.

6. Pour the sour salad dressing over the pineapple salad with avocado and celery and mix well. Then cover the bowl to place the salad in the fridge for few hours.

Nutritional Information:

Calories: 140; Total fat: 22 oz; Total carbohydrates: 35 oz; Protein: 11 oz

Pineapple, Avocado, and Honey Salad

 *Prep Time: 20 min. | Servings: 2*

Ingredients:

1 big and fresh pineapple, peeled and cubed

2 avocados, peeled and cubed

1 ripe orange, peeled and cubed

1 kiwi, peeled and cubed

5 tablespoons liquid honey

1 cup of bananas, cubed

5 tablespoons lemon juice

How to Prepare:

1. Pour 2 tablespoons of honey on top of the avocados, kiwi and orange cubes.

2. Add in the cubed banana and combine with the cubed pineapple, avocado, kiwi, orange cubes and honey to mix well.

3. After you combine all the pineapple salad ingredients pour the lemon juice and all the honey over the pineapple, avocado and honey salad and you are free to serve!

Nutritional Information:

Calories: 99; Total fat: 15 oz; Total carbohydrates: 26 oz; Protein: 8 oz

Pineapple, Avocado, and Mango Salad

 Prep Time: 20 min. | Servings: 2

Ingredients:

1 big and fresh pineapple, peeled and cubed

2 avocados, peeled and cubed

1 ripe mango, peeled and cubed

1 kiwi, peeled and cubed

5 tablespoons liquid honey

1 cup of bananas, cubed

5 tablespoons lemon juice

How to Prepare:

1. Pour 2 tablespoons of honey on top of the avocados, kiwi and mango cubes.

2. Add in the cubed banana and combine with the cubed pineapple, avocado, kiwi, mango cubes and honey to mix well.

3. After you combine all the pineapple salad ingredients pour the lemon juice and all the honey over the pineapple, avocado, and mango salad and you are free to serve!

Nutritional Information:

Calories: 99; Total fat: 15 oz; Total carbohydrates: 26 oz; Protein: 8 oz

Pineapple, Avocado and Apples Salad with Walnuts

Prep Time: 20 min. | Roasting Time: 10 min. | Servings: 2

Ingredients:

1 big and fresh pineapple, peeled and cubed

2 avocados, peeled and cubed

2 sour apples, peeled and cubed

1 cup of walnuts

1 kiwi, peeled and cubed

5 tablespoons liquid honey

1 cup of bananas, cubed

5 tablespoons lemon juice

How to Prepare:

1. Preheat the oven to 250°- 270° Fahrenheit and roast the walnuts in the oven for 10 minutes until lightly browned and crispy and then set aside to cool completely. Grind the walnuts using a food processor or blender.

2. Pour 2 tablespoons of honey on top of the avocados, kiwi and apple cubes.

3. Add in the cubed banana and combine with the cubed pineapple, avocado, kiwi, apple cubes, walnuts and honey to mix well.

4. After you combine all the pineapple salad ingredients pour the lemon juice and all the honey over the pineapple, avocado and apples salad and you are free to serve!

Nutritional Information:

Calories: 109; Total fat: 16 oz; Total carbohydrates: 28 oz; Protein: 10 oz

Pineapple, Avocado and Raspberry Salad

 Prep Time: 20 min. | Servings: 2

Ingredients:

1 big and fresh pineapple, peeled and cubed

2 avocados, peeled and cubed

2 sour apples, peeled and cubed

1 cup of raspberries

1 kiwi, peeled and cubed

5 tablespoons raspberry jam

1 cup of bananas, cubed

5 tablespoons orange juice

How to Prepare:

1. Pour 2 tablespoons of raspberry jam on top of the avocados, kiwi and apple cubes.

2. Add in the cubed banana and combine with the raspberries, cubed pineapple, avocado, kiwi, apple cubes and raspberry jam to mix well.

3. After you combine all the pineapple salad ingredients pour the orange juice and all the raspberry jam over the

pineapple, avocado and raspberry salad and you are free to serve!

Nutritional Information:

Calories: 112; Total fat: 17 oz; Total carbohydrates: 29 oz; Protein: 10 oz

Pineapple, Avocado and Strawberry Salad

 Prep Time: 20 min. | Servings: 2

Ingredients:

1 big and fresh pineapple, peeled and cubed

2 avocados, peeled and cubed

2 sour apples, peeled and cubed

1 cup of strawberries

1 kiwi, peeled and cubed

1 cup of strawberry jam

1 cup of bananas, cubed

5 tablespoons orange juice

How to Prepare:

1. Pour 3 tablespoons of strawberry jam on top of the avocados, kiwi and apple cubes.

2. Add in the cubed banana and combine with the strawberries, cubed pineapple, avocado, kiwi, apple cubes and strawberry jam to mix well.

3. After you combine all the pineapple salad ingredients pour the orange juice and all the strawberry jam over the

pineapple, avocado and strawberry salad and you are free to serve!

Nutritional Information:

Calories: 114; Total fat: 18 oz; Total carbohydrates: 30 oz; Protein: 12 oz

Pineapple, Avocado and Cherry Salad

 Prep Time: 20 min. | Servings: 2

Ingredients:

1 big and fresh pineapple, peeled and cubed

2 avocados, peeled and cubed

2 sour apples, peeled and cubed

2 cups of cherries, pitted

1 kiwi, peeled and cubed

1 cup of cherry jam

1 cup of bananas, cubed

5 tablespoons orange juice

1 teaspoon pure vanilla extract

Chocolate spray cream

How to Prepare:

1. Pour 3 tablespoons of cherry jam on top of the avocados, kiwi and apple cubes.

2. Add in the cubed banana and combine with the cherries, cubed pineapple, avocado, kiwi, apple cubes and cherry jam to mix well.

3. After you combine all the pineapple salad ingredients pour the orange juice and all the cherry jam over the pineapple, avocado and cherry salad. Add in the chocolate spray cream on top and you are free to serve!

Nutritional Information:

Calories: 116; Total fat: 19 oz; Total carbohydrates: 31 oz; Protein: 11 oz

Pineapple Salad with Cucumbers and Feta Cheese

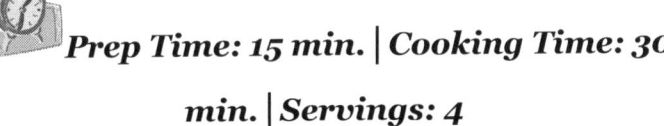**Prep Time: 15 min. | Cooking Time: 30 min. | Servings: 4**

Ingredients:

1 can of canned pineapple chunks, cubed

1 cup of Feta cheese, crumbled

2 cucumbers, peeled and cubed

1 beet

1 cup of green Olives, pitted

1 cup of raisins

salt and pepper

fresh chives, chopped

Dressing:

2 tablespoons Olive oil

5 tablespoons mayonnaise

5 garlic cloves

4 tablespoons mustard

salt and pepper to taste

How to Prepare:

1. Soak the raisins in the warm water for 10 minutes.

2. Place the beet in a saucepan with the water and boil over medium heat for around 30 minutes until soft. Then cool the beet by placing in the cold water for 5 minutes and then peel and cube it.

3. In a bowl, combine the pineapple chunks, raisins, beet, cucumber, olives, Feta cheese, salt, pepper, and chopped chives.

4. Let's get to the dressing now - beat all the dressing ingredients in a food processor until they have a smooth and creamy consistency.

5. Spoon the dressing over the salad and then mix well.

6. Place the pineapple salad with the cucumbers and Feta cheese in the fridge for 1 hour and then serve.

Nutritional Information:

Calories: 177; Total fat: 17 oz; Total carbohydrates: 33 oz; Protein:

12 oz

Pineapple Salad with Cucumbers and Tomato

 Prep Time: 20 min. | Cooking Time: 30 min. | Servings: 4

Ingredients:

1 can of canned pineapple chunks, cubed

1 cup of Feta cheese, crumbled

2 cucumbers, peeled and cubed

3 medium tomatoes, cubed

1 beet

1 cup of black Olives, pitted

1 cup of dried apricots, cubed

salt and pepper

fresh parsley, chopped

Dressing:

2 tablespoons Olive oil

5 tablespoons mayonnaise

5 garlic cloves

4 tablespoons mustard

salt and pepper to taste

How to Prepare:

1. Soak the apricots in the warm water for 10 minutes and then chop them.

2. Place the beet in a saucepan with the water and boil over medium heat for around 30 minutes until soft. Then cool the beet by placing it in the cold water for 5 minutes and then peel and cube it.

3. In a bowl, combine the pineapple chunks, apricots, beet, cucumbers, tomatoes, olives, Feta cheese, salt, pepper, and chopped parsley.

4. Let's get to the dressing now - beat all the dressing ingredients in a food processor until they have a smooth and creamy consistency.

5. Spoon the dressing over the salad and then mix well. After that place the pineapple salad with the cucumbers and tomatoes in the fridge for 1 hour and then serve.

Nutritional Information:

Calories: 175; Total fat: 16 oz; Total carbohydrates: 32 oz; Protein: 13 oz

Pineapple Salad with Cucumbers and Hazelnuts

Prep Time: 20 min. | Cooking Time: 40 min. | Servings: 4

Ingredients:

1 can of canned pineapple chunks, cubed

1 cup of hazelnuts

1 cup of Feta cheese, crumbled

2 cucumbers, peeled and cubed

1 cup of cherry tomatoes, halved

1 beet

1 cup of black Olives, pitted

1 cup of dried apricots, cubed

salt and pepper

fresh parsley, chopped

Dressing:

5 tablespoons Olive oil

How to Prepare:

1. Soak the apricots in the warm water for 10 minutes and then chop them.

2. Preheat the oven to 250°- 270° Fahrenheit and roast the hazelnuts in the oven for 10 minutes until lightly browned and crispy and then set aside to cool completely. Then grind the hazelnuts using a food processor or blender.

3. Place the beet in a saucepan with the water and boil over medium heat for around 30 minutes until soft. Then cool the beet by placing it in the cold water for 5 minutes and then peel and cube it.

4. In a bowl, combine the pineapple chunks, apricots, beet, cucumbers, tomatoes, olives, Feta cheese, hazelnuts, salt, pepper, and chopped parsley.

5. Spoon the Olive oil over the salad and then mix well. After that place the pineapple salad with cucumbers and hazelnuts in the fridge for 1 hour and only then serve.

Nutritional Information:

Calories: 176; Total fat: 17 oz; Total carbohydrates: 34 oz; Protein: 14 oz

Pineapple and Melon Salad with Walnuts

 Prep Time: 20 min. | Roasting Time: 10 min. | Servings: 4

Ingredients:

1 fresh pineapple, peeled and cubed

1 sweet melon, peeled and cubed

1 cup of walnuts

2 cups of raisins

5 oz lettuce, chopped

1 cup of arugula

5 tablespoons lemon juice

3 tablespoons maple syrup

How to Prepare:

1. Preheat the oven to 250°- 270° Fahrenheit and roast the walnuts in the oven for 10 minutes until lightly browned and crispy and then set aside to cool completely. Then grind the walnuts using a food processor or blender.

2. Soak the raisins in the warm water for 10 minutes.

3. Combine the lettuce and arugula with the cubed melon. Cube the pineapple chunks as well.

4. Combine all the ingredients and pour the lemon juice and maple syrup over the salad.

5. Place the pineapple and melon salad in the fridge for 1 hour and then serve.

Nutritional Information:

Calories: 167; Total fat: 15 oz; Total carbohydrates: 28 oz; Protein: 12 oz

Pineapple and Melon Salad with Cashews

Prep Time: 20 min. | Roasting Time: 10 min. | Servings: 4

Ingredients:

1 fresh pineapple, peeled and cubed

1 sweet melon, peeled and cubed

1 cup of cashews

2 cups of raisins

5 oz lettuce, chopped

5 tablespoons lemon juice

3 tablespoons maple syrup

How to Prepare:

1. Preheat the oven to 250°- 270° Fahrenheit and roast the cashews in the oven for 10 minutes until lightly browned and crispy and then set aside to cool completely.

2. Soak the raisins in the warm water for 10 minutes.

3. Combine the lettuce with the cubed melon and the pineapple chunks as well.

4. Combine all the ingredients and pour the lemon juice and maple syrup over the salad.

5. Place the pineapple and melon salad in the fridge for 1 hour and then serve.

Nutritional Information:

Calories: 165; Total fat: 14 oz; Total carbohydrates: 27 oz; Protein: 11 oz

Pineapple and Melon Salad with Strawberries

 Prep Time: 20 min. | Servings: 4

Ingredients:

1 fresh pineapple, peeled and cubed

1 sweet and medium melon, peeled and cubed

1 cup of small strawberries

2 kiwi's, peeled and cubed

1 cup of raisins

5 tablespoons lemon juice

3 tablespoons strawberry jam

How to Prepare:

1. Soak the raisins in the warm water for 10 minutes.

2. Combine the cubed melon and the pineapple chunks with the raisins, kiwi's and strawberries.

3. Combine all the ingredients and pour the lemon juice and spoon the strawberry jam over the salad.

4. Place the pineapple and melon salad with strawberries in the fridge for 1 hour and then serve with the spray cream on top.

Nutritional Information:

Calories: 165; Total fat: 14 oz; Total carbohydrates: 27 oz; Protein:

11 oz

Spiralized Pineapple Salad with Celery and Walnuts

 Prep Time: 20 min. | Servings: 4

Ingredients:

1 big and fresh pineapple, peeled

1 cup of walnuts

4 celery stalks, cubed

4 tomatoes, cubed

fresh basil

Dressing:

4 tablespoons Olive oil

4 garlic cloves

1 teaspoon chili powder

2 teaspoons lemon juice

Sea salt and pepper to taste

How to Prepare:

1. Preheat the oven to 270°- 300° Fahrenheit and roast the walnuts in the oven for 10 minutes until lightly browned and

crispy. Then grind the walnuts using a food processor or blender.

2. Spiralize or grate the pineapple in Korean style using a Korean carrot grater.

3. Combine the cubed celery stalks with the pineapple, tomatoes, and walnuts.

4. Let's get to the sauce now – combine the olive oil, garlic, chili powder, lemon juice, salt, and pepper and beat all ingredients in a blender.

5. Pour the pineapple salad dressing over the pineapple salad and add the fresh basil on top! Serve this delicious pineapple salad with the cold lemonade.

Nutritional Information:

Calories: 153; Total fat: 13 oz; Total carbohydrates: 17 oz; Protein: 9 oz

Spiralized Pineapple Salad with Cucumbers and Hazelnuts

 Prep Time: 20 min. | Servings: 4

Ingredients:

1 big and fresh pineapple, peeled

1 cup of hazelnuts

2 cucumbers, peeled and cubed

1 pear, peeled and cubed

fresh basil

Dressing:

4 tablespoons Olive oil

4 garlic cloves

1 teaspoon chili powder

4 teaspoons orange juice, freshly squeezed

Sea salt and pepper to taste

How to Prepare:

1. Preheat the oven to 270°- 300° Fahrenheit and roast the hazelnuts in the oven for 10 minutes until lightly browned

and crispy. Then grind the hazelnuts using a food processor or blender.

2. Spiralize or grate the pineapple in Korean style using a Korean carrot grater.

3. Combine the cubed cucumbers with the pineapple, pear, and hazelnuts.

4. Let's get to the sauce now – combine the olive oil, garlic, chili powder, orange juice, salt, and pepper and beat all ingredients in a blender.

5. Pour the pineapple salad dressing over the pineapple salad and add the fresh basil on top! Serve this delicious pineapple salad with the cold lemonade.

Nutritional Information:

Calories: 151; Total fat: 14 oz; Total carbohydrates: 18 oz; Protein: 10 oz

Prep Time: 20 min. | Servings: 4

Ingredients:

1 big and fresh pineapple, peeled

1 cup of cashews

4 oranges, peeled and cubed

3 pears, peeled and cubed

Dressing:

4 tablespoons orange juice

1 teaspoon pure vanilla extract

How to Prepare:

1. Preheat the oven to 270°- 300° Fahrenheit and roast the cashews in the oven for 10 minutes until lightly browned and crispy. Then grind the cashews using a food processor.

2. Spiralize or grate the pineapple in Korean style using a Korean carrot grater.

3. Combine the cubed oranges with the pineapple, pears, and cashews.

4. Let's get to the sauce now – combine the orange juice with the pure vanilla extract and beat all ingredients in a blender.

5. Pour the pineapple salad dressing over the pineapple salad! Serve this delicious pineapple salad with the spray cream and cold lemonade.

Nutritional Information:

Calories: 149; Total fat: 12 oz; Total carbohydrates: 18 oz; Protein: 10 oz

Spiralized Pineapple Salad with Grapes and Walnuts

 Prep Time: 15 min. | Roasting Time: 10 min. | Servings: 3

Ingredients:

1 big and fresh pineapple, peeled

2 cups of sweet grapes

2 sour apples, peeled

1 cup of walnuts

2 kiwis, peeled and cubed

Cinnamon

Dressing:

4 tablespoons liquid honey

1 teaspoon pure vanilla extract

How to Prepare:

1. Spiralize or grate the pineapple and apples in Korean style using a Korean carrot grater.

2. Combine the cubed kiwis with the pineapple, apples and grapes.

3. Meanwhile, preheat the oven to 250°- 270° Fahrenheit and roast the walnuts in the oven for 10 minutes until lightly browned and crispy. Then grind the walnuts.

4. Let's get to the sauce now – combine the liquid honey with the pure vanilla extract and beat all ingredients in a blender.

5. Pour the pineapple salad dressing over the pineapple salad and sprinkle some cinnamon on top! Serve this delicious pineapple salad with the spray cream.

Nutritional Information:

Calories: 149; Total fat: 14 oz; Total carbohydrates: 19 oz; Protein: 9 oz

Sweet Pineapple, Melon and Pears Salad with Blueberries

*Prep Time: 30 min. | Servings: 5*

Ingredients:

1 big and fresh pineapple, peeled and cubed

3 cups of melon, peeled and cubed

3 cups of pears, peeled and cubed

1 cup of blueberries

5 tablespoons liquid honey

How to Prepare:

1. In a bowl, combine the cubed pineapple, melon, pears and blueberries.

2. Mix all the fruits well and spoon the honey over the salad.

3. Place the pineapple, melon and pears salad in the fridge for 1 hour and then serve with the spray cream on top.

Nutritional Information:

Calories: 149; Total fat: 13 oz; Total carbohydrates: 25 oz; Protein: 9 oz

Pineapple Salad with Mango and Peanuts

 Prep Time: 25 min. | Roasting Time: 10 min. | Servings: 5

Ingredients:

1 fresh pineapple, peeled and cubed

2 mangos, peeled and cubed

2 cups of peanuts

1 cup of raisins

3 tablespoons liquid honey

3 tablespoons lemon juice

How to Prepare:

1. Preheat the oven to 260°- 290° Fahrenheit and roast the peanuts in the oven for 10 minutes until lightly browned and crispy. Then grind the peanuts.

2. Wash and soak the raisins in the warm water for 10 minutes.

3. Combine the cubed pineapple with the cubed mangos and roasted peanuts.

4. Add in the raisins and spoon the liquid honey with the lemon juice over the pineapple, mango and peanuts salad. Serve with the chocolate spray cream on top.

Nutritional Information:

Calories: 168; Total fat: 13 oz; Total carbohydrates: 19 oz; Protein:

12 oz

Prep Time: 20 min. | Roasting Time: 10 min. | Servings: 4

Ingredients:

1 big and fresh pineapple, peeled and cubed

3 cups of cherries, pitted

1 cup of walnuts

1 cup of raisins

4 tablespoons pumpkin seeds

5 tablespoons liquid honey

5 tablespoons lemon juice

How to Prepare:

1. Preheat the oven to 270°- 290° Fahrenheit and roast the walnuts in the oven for 10 minutes until lightly browned and crispy and then set aside to cool completely. Then grind the walnuts.
2. Wash and soak the raisins in the warm water for 10 minutes.
3. Combine the cubed pineapple with the cherries and roasted walnuts.

4. Mix in the raisins and pumpkin seeds. Now pour the liquid honey and lemon juice over the pineapple, walnuts and cherries salad. Then add the chocolate cream on top and serve.

Nutritional Information:

Calories: 177; Total fat: 14 oz; Total carbohydrates: 19 oz; Protein: 12 oz

Prep Time: 20 min. | Roasting Time: 10 min. | Servings: 4

Ingredients:

1 big and fresh pineapple, peeled and cubed

3 cups of plums, pitted and cubed

1 cup of cashews

1 cup of raisins

4 tablespoons pumpkin seeds

5 tablespoons liquid honey

5 tablespoons lemon juice

How to Prepare:

1. Preheat the oven to 270°- 290° Fahrenheit and roast the cashews in the oven for 10 minutes until lightly browned and crispy and then set aside to cool completely.

2. Wash and soak the raisins in the warm water for 10 minutes.

3. Combine the cubed pineapple with the plums and roasted cashews.

4. Mix in the raisins and pumpkin seeds. Now pour the liquid honey and lemon juice over the pineapple, cashews and plums salad. Then add the chocolate cream on top and serve.

Nutritional Information:

Calories: 179; Total fat: 15 oz; Total carbohydrates: 21 oz; Protein: 13 oz

Pineapple and Almonds Salad with Raspberries

 Prep Time: 20 min. | Roasting Time: 10 min. | Servings: 4

Ingredients:

1 pineapple, peeled and cubed

2 cups of fresh raspberries

5 strawberries

1 cup of almonds

1 cup of raisins

4 tablespoons sunflower seeds

5 tablespoons liquid honey

5 tablespoons orange juice

How to Prepare:

1. Preheat the oven to 270°- 290° Fahrenheit and roast the almonds in the oven for 10 minutes until lightly browned and crispy and then set aside to cool completely. Grind the almonds.

2. Wash and soak the raisins in the warm water for 10 minutes.

3. Combine the cubed pineapple with the raspberries, strawberries and roasted almonds.

4. Mix in the raisins and sunflower seeds. Now pour the liquid honey and orange juice over the pineapple, almonds and raspberries salad. Then add the chocolate cream on top and serve.

Nutritional Information:

Calories: 178; Total fat: 14 oz; Total carbohydrates: 20 oz; Protein: 12 oz

Chapter III: Hot Dishes

Baked Pineapple with Beef and Potatoes

 Prep Time: 20 min. | Cooking Time: 60 min. | Servings: 4

Ingredients:

4 cups of fresh pineapple, peeled and cubed

20 oz beef, cubed

5 medium potatoes, peeled and cubed

1 chili pepper

1 red onion, peeled and chopped

10 cloves of garlic, chopped

4 tablespoons garlic powder

7 tablespoons of Olive oil

4 teaspoons lemon juice

salt and pepper

basil

How to Prepare:

1. Combine the pineapple and beef with the chili pepper, chopped garlic and onion. Add in some lemon juice.
2. Preheat the oven to 280°-300° Fahrenheit and bake the pineapple and beef with the potatoes, oil, garlic powder, garlic, onion, salt, pepper and basil for 45-60 minutes until the beef meat is soft.
3. Pour the lemon juice over the baked pineapple, beef and potatoes and then serve.

Nutritional Information:

Calories: 319; Total fat: 38 oz; Total carbohydrates: 57 oz; Protein: 27 oz

Prep Time: 20 min. | Cooking Time: 60 min. | Servings: 4

Ingredients:

4 cups of fresh pineapple, peeled and cubed

20 oz pork, cubed

5 medium potatoes, peeled and cubed

1 chili pepper

1 red onion, peeled and chopped

10 cloves of garlic, chopped

4 tablespoons garlic powder

7 tablespoons of sunflower oil

4 teaspoons lemon juice

salt and pepper

basil

How to Prepare:

1. Combine the pineapple and pork with the chili pepper, chopped garlic and onion. Add in some lemon juice.

2. Preheat the oven to 280°-300° Fahrenheit and bake the pineapple and pork with the potatoes, oil, garlic powder, garlic, onion, salt, pepper and basil for 45-60 minutes until the pork meat is soft.

3. Pour the lemon juice over the baked pineapple, pork and potatoes and then serve.

Nutritional Information:

Calories: 329; Total fat: 39 oz; Total carbohydrates: 59 oz; Protein: 29 oz

Prep Time: 20 min. | Cooking Time: 45 min. | Servings: 4

Ingredients:

4 cups of fresh pineapple, peeled and cubed

4 hakes, cubed

5 carrots, peeled and spiralized

5 medium potatoes, peeled and cubed

1 chili pepper

1 red onion, peeled and chopped

10 cloves of garlic, chopped

4 tablespoons garlic powder

7 tablespoons of sunflower oil

4 teaspoons lemon juice

salt and pepper

basil

How to Prepare:

1. Defrost the hake and then combine the pineapple and hake with the chili pepper, chopped garlic and onion. Add in some lemon juice.

2. Preheat the oven to 280°-300° Fahrenheit and bake the pineapple and hake with the potatoes, oil, garlic powder, garlic, onion, salt, pepper and basil for 35-45 minutes until the fish is soft.

3. Pour the lemon juice over the baked pineapple, hake and carrots and then serve.

Nutritional Information:

Calories: 299; Total fat: 30 oz; Total carbohydrates: 44 oz; Protein: 22 oz

Prep Time: 20 min. | Cooking Time: 55 min. | Servings: 4

Ingredients:

4 cups of fresh pineapple, peeled and cubed

4 hakes, cubed

2 cups of pumpkin, peeled and cubed

5 medium potatoes, peeled and cubed

1 chili pepper

1 red onion, peeled and chopped

10 cloves of garlic, chopped

4 tablespoons garlic powder

7 tablespoons of sunflower oil

4 teaspoons lemon juice

salt and pepper

basil

How to Prepare:

1. Defrost the hake and then combine the pineapple and hake with the chili pepper, chopped garlic and onion. Add in some lemon juice.

2. Heat the wok or frying pan and fry the pumpkin cubes for 10 minutes.

3. Preheat the oven to 280°-300° Fahrenheit and bake the pineapple and hake with the pumpkin, potatoes, oil, garlic powder, garlic, onion, salt, pepper and basil for 35-45 minutes until the fish is soft.

4. Pour the lemon juice over the baked pineapple, hake and pumpkin cubes and then serve.

Nutritional Information:

Calories: 290; Total fat: 31 oz; Total carbohydrates: 45 oz; Protein: 21 oz

Pineapple with Baked Hake and Zucchini

 Prep Time: 20 min. | Cooking Time: 55 min. | Servings: 4

Ingredients:

4 cups of fresh pineapple, peeled and cubed

4 hakes, cubed

1 zucchini, peeled and spiralized

5 medium potatoes, peeled and cubed

1 chili pepper

1 red onion, peeled and chopped

10 cloves of garlic, chopped

4 tablespoons garlic powder

7 tablespoons of sunflower oil

4 teaspoons lemon juice

salt and pepper

basil

How to Prepare:

1. Defrost the hake and then combine the pineapple and hake with the chili pepper, chopped garlic and onion. Add in some lemon juice.

2. Heat the wok or frying pan and then fry the zucchini for 10 minutes.

3. Preheat the oven to 280°-300° Fahrenheit and bake the pineapple and hake with the zucchini, potatoes, oil, garlic powder, garlic, onion, salt, pepper and basil for 35-45 minutes until the fish is soft.

4. Pour the lemon juice over the baked pineapple, hake and zucchini and then serve.

Nutritional Information:

Calories: 292; Total fat: 33 oz; Total carbohydrates: 44 oz; Protein: 20 oz

Prep Time: 20 min. | Cooking Time: 55 min. | Servings: 4

Ingredients:

4 cups of fresh pineapple, peeled and cubed

4 hakes, cubed

4 cups of squash, peeled and cubed

5 medium potatoes, peeled and cubed

1 chili pepper

1 red onion, peeled and chopped

10 cloves of garlic, chopped

4 tablespoons garlic powder

7 tablespoons of Olive oil

5 tablespoons mayonnaise

4 teaspoons lemon juice

salt and pepper

How to Prepare:

1. Defrost the hake and then combine the pineapple and hake with the salt, chili pepper, chopped garlic and onion. Add in

some lemon juice and mayonnaise. Marinate the hake for few hours.

2. Heat the wok or frying pan and fry the squash cubes for 10 minutes.

3. Preheat the oven to 280°-300° Fahrenheit and bake the pineapple and hake with the squash, potatoes, oil, garlic powder, garlic, onion, salt, pepper and basil for 35-45 minutes until the fish is soft.

4. Pour the lemon juice over the baked pineapple, hake and squash cubes and then serve.

Nutritional Information:

Calories: 295; Total fat: 32 oz; Total carbohydrates: 46 oz; Protein: 22 oz

Turkey in Mayonnaise and Pineapples

Prep Time: 20 min. | Cooking Time: 40-50 min. | Servings:

5

Ingredients:

1 big and fresh pineapple, peeled and cubed

20 oz turkey breast, cubed

2 cups of mayonnaise

2 onions, peeled and chopped

5 tomatoes, cubed

6 tablespoons Olive oil

4 tablespoons soy sauce

4 tablespoons freshly squeezed lemon juice

1/2 teaspoon powdered chili pepper

2 tablespoons powdered garlic

salt and pepper

How to Prepare:

1. In a bowl, combine powdered chili pepper, powdered garlic, and some salt. Season the turkey cubes with the salt and pepper, and toss in the powdered garlic and powdered chili pepper mix. Combine the mayonnaise and cubed pineapples with the meat and marinate the turkey breast for 3 hours.

2. Heat the oil in a skillet and stew the cubed turkey breast with the closed lid for around 30-50 minutes until golden brown and soft. Few minutes before the turkey is ready mix in the chopped onions, and stew the turkey cubes for 10 minutes more. Combine the soy sauce with the cubed tomatoes and spoon over the turkey.

3. Sprinkle the salt and pepper and pour the freshly squeezed lemon juice over the turkey breast and you are free to serve the turkey meat in separate dishes. Remember that this dish should be served warm.

Nutritional Information:

Calories: 340; Total fat: 57 oz; Total carbohydrates: 72 oz; Protein: 35 oz

Turkey, Pineapples and Bell Peppers

Prep Time: 20 min. | Cooking Time: 60 min. | Servings: 3

Ingredients:

1 big and fresh pineapple, peeled and cubed

15 oz turkey breast, cubed

2 red bell peppers, cubed

2 orange bell peppers

3 onions, peeled and chopped

4 tomatoes, cubed

7 tablespoons sunflower oil

4 tablespoons soy sauce

5 garlic cloves, minced

2 tablespoons powdered garlic

salt and pepper

How to Prepare:

1. In a bowl, combine the powdered garlic, minced garlic, and some salt. Season the turkey cubes with the salt and pepper, and toss in the garlic mix. Combine the tomatoes and cubed pineapples with the turkey meat and marinate the turkey breast for 5 hours.

2. Heat the oil in a skillet and stew the cubed turkey breast with the closed lid for around 30-50 minutes until golden brown and soft. Few minutes before the turkey is ready mix in the chopped onions and bell peppers and stew the turkey cubes for 20 minutes more.

3. Sprinkle the salt and pepper and pour the soy sauce over the turkey breast and you are free to serve the turkey meat in separate dishes. Remember that this dish should be served warm.

Nutritional Information:

Calories: 349; Total fat: 53 oz; Total carbohydrates: 69 oz; Protein: 32 oz

Chapter IV: Pineapple Pies

Pineapple Pie with Toffees

Prep Time: 15 min. | Baking Time: 1 hour | Servings: 5

Ingredients:

9" or 11" in diameter pie crust (pastry shell)

1 big and fresh pineapple, peeled and grated

2 cups of toffee bits, chopped

2 cups of sugar

3 tablespoons pineapple jam

1 teaspoon cinnamon

½ teaspoon cloves, ground

10 oz unsalted butter

How to Prepare:

1. In a saucepan, combine the pineapples, sugar, butter, cinnamon and cloves and stew for around 20 minutes over low heat with the closed lid until the smooth consistency. Spoon the pineapple jam over the mixture.

2. Spoon the pineapple mixture into the pastry shell and add one cup of the toffees on top, and then bake for 40 minutes.

3. 10 minutes before the pineapple pie is ready open the oven and spoon one cup of toffee bits on top. Serve with the spray cream and coffee.

Nutritional Information:

Calories: 151; Total fat: 22 oz; Total carbohydrates: 34 oz; Protein: 14 oz

Pineapple Pie with Apples and Toffees

Prep Time: 15 min. | Baking Time: 1 hour | Servings: 5

Ingredients:

9" or 11" in diameter pie crust (pastry shell)

1 big and fresh pineapple, peeled and grated

5 sour apples, peeled and cubed

2 cups of toffee bits, chopped

1 cup of sugar

1 teaspoon cinnamon

½ teaspoon cloves, ground

10 oz unsalted butter

How to Prepare:

1. In a saucepan, combine the pineapples, sugar, butter, cinnamon and cloves and stew for around 20 minutes over low heat with the closed lid until the smooth consistency. Mix in the cubed apples.

2. Spoon the pineapple and apples mixture into the pastry shell and add one cup of the toffees on top, and then bake for around 40 minutes.

3. 10 minutes before the pineapple and apples pie is ready open the oven and spoon one cup of toffee bits on top. Serve with the spray cream and coffee.

Nutritional Information:

Calories: 159; Total fat: 24 oz; Total carbohydrates: 39 oz; Protein: 17 oz

Pineapple Pie with Pears and Toffees

Prep Time: 15 min. | Baking Time: 1 hour | Servings: 5

Ingredients:

9" or 11" in diameter pie crust (pastry shell)

1 big and fresh pineapple, peeled and grated

5 sweet and juicy pears, peeled and cubed

2 cups of toffee bits, chopped

1 cup of sugar

1 teaspoon vanilla

½ teaspoon cloves, ground

10 oz unsalted butter

How to Prepare:

1. In a saucepan, combine the pineapples, sugar, butter, vanilla and cloves and stew for around 20 minutes over low heat with the closed lid until the smooth consistency. Mix in the cubed pears.

2. Spoon the pineapple and pears mixture into the pastry shell and add one cup of the toffees on top, and then bake for around 40 minutes.

3. 10 minutes before the pineapple and pears pie is ready open the oven and spoon one cup of toffee bits on top. Serve with the spray cream and coffee.

Nutritional Information:

Calories: 157; Total fat: 23 oz; Total carbohydrates: 37 oz; Protein: 16 oz

Pineapple Pie with Walnuts and Toffees

Prep Time: 15 min. | Baking Time: 1 hour | Servings: 4

Ingredients:

9" or 11" in diameter pie crust (pastry shell)

1 big and fresh pineapple, peeled and grated

1 cup of walnuts

5 sour apples, peeled and cubed

2 cups of toffee bits, chopped

1 cup of sugar

1 teaspoon cinnamon

½ teaspoon cloves, ground

10 oz unsalted butter

How to Prepare:

1. Preheat the oven to 250°- 270° Fahrenheit and roast the walnuts in the oven for 10 minutes until lightly browned and crispy and then set aside to cool completely. Then grind the walnuts using a food processor or blender

2. In a saucepan, combine the pineapples, sugar, butter, cinnamon and cloves and stew for around 20 minutes over low heat with the closed lid until the smooth consistency. Mix in the cubed apples and walnuts.

3. Spoon the pineapple and walnuts mixture into the pastry shell and add one cup of the toffees on top, and then bake for around 40 minutes.

4. 10 minutes before the pineapple and walnuts pie is ready open the oven and spoon one cup of toffee bits on top. Serve with the spray cream and cocoa.

Nutritional Information:

Calories: 159; Total fat: 24 oz; Total carbohydrates: 39 oz; Protein: 17 oz

Chocolate Pineapple Pie with Walnuts

Prep Time: 15 min. | Baking Time: 1 hour | Servings: 4

Ingredients:

9" in diameter pie crust (pastry shell)

2 fresh pineapples, peeled and cubed

1 cup of walnuts

2 cups of dark chocolate

2 cups of toffee bits, chopped

1 cup of sugar

1 teaspoon cinnamon

½ teaspoon cloves, ground

10 oz unsalted butter

How to Prepare:

1. Preheat the oven to 250°- 270° Fahrenheit and roast the walnuts in the oven for 10 minutes until lightly browned and crispy and then set aside to cool completely. Then grind the walnuts using a food processor or blender

2. In a saucepan, combine the pineapples, sugar, butter, cinnamon and cloves and stew for around 20 minutes over low heat with the closed lid until the smooth consistency. Then add in the walnuts and chocolate cubes.

3. Spoon the pineapple, chocolate and walnuts mixture into the pastry shell and add one cup of the toffees on top, and then bake for around 40 minutes.

4. 10 minutes before the pineapple and walnuts pie is ready open the oven and spoon one cup of toffee bits on top. Serve with the spray cream and cocoa.

Nutritional Information:

Calories: 161; Total fat: 25 oz; Total carbohydrates: 40 oz; Protein: 18 oz

Pineapple Pie with Hazelnuts

Prep Time: 15 min. | Baking Time: 1 h | Servings: 6

Ingredients:

2 cups of wheat flour

2 teaspoons baking powder

1 teaspoon vanilla

2 cups of unsalted butter

1 teaspoon baking spray

Filling:

2 medium pineapples, peeled and grated

1 cup of wheat flour

2 cups of sugar

1 teaspoon cinnamon

1 cup of cream

half cup walnuts

How to Prepare:

1. Preheat the oven to 240°-260° Fahrenheit and roast the walnuts in the oven until golden brown and crispy and then coat the pie pan with the baking spray or butter and leave it in the oven to melt the butter.

2. In a big bowl, combine the pineapples with 1 cup of the sugar and leave for 15 minutes.

3. In a second bowl, combine the flour, baking powder, butter and vanilla and mix well.

4. Blend the mixture with the water until the dough has a smooth consistency and then pin out the dough and place it into the pie pan.

5. Let's prepare the pie filling now – combine the flour with the sugar, cinnamon, 1/3 of pineapples and walnuts.

6. Spoon 1/3 of the pineapples on the crust and then spoon half of the flour mixture on top. Top with the grated pineapples and second part of the flour mixture. Pour the cream and place the butter slices on top.

7. Place the pineapple pie into the oven and bake for 1 hour until the top of the pie is golden brown and crispy.

Nutritional Information:

Calories: 205; Total fat: 28 oz; Total carbohydrates: 42 oz; Protein: 21 oz

Pineapple Pie with Oranges and Toffees

Prep Time: 15 min. | Baking Time: 1 hour | Servings: 4

Ingredients:

9" or 11" in diameter pie crust (pastry shell)

1 big and fresh pineapple, peeled and cubed

3 cups of oranges, peeled and cubed

1 cup of hazelnuts

2 cups of toffee bits, chopped

2 cups of sugar

1 teaspoon cinnamon

½ teaspoon cloves, ground

1 cup of unsalted butter

How to Prepare:

1. Preheat the oven to 250°- 270° Fahrenheit and roast the hazelnuts in the oven for 10 minutes until lightly browned and crispy and then set aside to cool completely. Then grind the hazelnuts using a food processor or blender

2. In a saucepan, combine the pineapples, sugar, butter, cinnamon, oranges and cloves and stew for around 20 minutes over low heat with the closed lid. Mix in the hazelnuts.

3. Spoon the pineapple and oranges mixture into the pastry shell and add one cup of the toffees on top, and then bake for around 40 minutes.

4. 10 minutes before the pineapple and oranges pie is ready open the oven and spoon one cup of toffee bits on top. Serve with the spray cream and cocoa.

Nutritional Information:

Calories: 158; Total fat: 23 oz; Total carbohydrates: 38 oz; Protein: 16 oz

Conclusion

Thank you for buying this third pineapple cookbook. I hope this book was able to help you prepare tasty and healthy pineapple salads, soups or pies.

If you've enjoyed this book, I'd greatly appreciate if you could leave your honest opinion.

Your direct feedback could be used to help other readers to discover the advantages of pineapple recipes!

Thank you again and I hope you have enjoyed this cookbook.

Recipe Index

Printed in Great Britain
by Amazon

35025848R00066